The Ultimate Cookbook for Teens:

365 Days of Delicious, Budget-Friendly, and Quick Recipes Tailored for Young Chefs with Guidance from a Top Culinary Expert!

By:
Elara Stormveil

Table of Contents

Introduction

The kitchen is an often-overlooked area that has enormous power to influence and enhance this critical stage of life in the busy world of adolescence, where school, friendships, and self-discovery intersect. Welcome to the "Teens' Cookbook," a culinary adventure created especially for teenagers who want to master the art of cooking and set off on a savory voyage that bridges the gap between processed foods and home-cooked treats.

Teenage years are a time of discovery, personal development, and independence. During this stage, people start to establish their identities, nurture their passions, and build the abilities necessary to succeed as adults. However, young people are more likely to rely on fast food, packaged snacks, and takeaway as the pressures of everyday life increase. By enabling teens to take charge of their nutrition, health, and creativity in the comfort of their own homes, the "Teens' Cookbook" aims to shift this narrative.

We shall explore the world of cooking in this cookbook while keeping in mind the goals, preferences, and time constraints of teenagers. We are aware that time can be a valuable resource, and that the kitchen's variety of tools, foods, and cooking methods might be intimidating. Fear not, for you will discover a range of recipes in these pages that are not only tasty and nourishing, but also created for the inexperienced cook. This cookbook will walk you through step-by-step instructions for recipes that celebrate the delights of cooking while honoring the reality of a hectic adolescent life, from quick weekday breakfasts to leisurely weekend gatherings, from savory comfort foods to decadent desserts.

The "Teens' Cookbook" is a resource for learning critical life skills rather than only a collection of recipes. You'll learn about food safety, fundamentals of nutrition, and the science behind cooking processes as you hone your cooking skills. Your dishes will be improved if you understand how components work together and how different flavors enhance one another. This will also help you develop a greater appreciation for the culinary arts.

In addition to teaching useful skills, this cookbook promotes experimentation and creativity. We are aware that every person has different dietary requirements and taste preferences. As a result, you'll find modifications, swaps, and advice to help you tailor each recipe to your own tastes. You might even start coming up with your own unique recipes that express your personality and cooking flair as you develop more confidence in the kitchen.

The act of cooking invites one to connect, explore, and nourishes both body and spirit. You can unplug from technology and focus on the here and now when you are cooking a meal. Sharing a home-cooked dinner with loved ones strengthens bonds and forges enduring memories. One recipe at a time, the "Teens' Cookbook" invites you to relish these experiences.

So, whether you're a total newbie or have some cooking experience, the "Teens' Cookbook" is your dependable travel partner on this fascinating culinary adventure. Remember that cooking is more than just a chore; it's a creative outlet, a way to express yourself, and a life skill that will be used for years to come as you turn the pages and go on a series of culinary adventures. Open your arms to the kitchen and let's go on this delicious adventure together.

Chapter 1:
Cooking for Teens

Setting Up Your Station

Always begin in a spotless kitchen. You may prevent infection and avert accidents in the kitchen by keeping it clean. So that you may often wash and dry your hands, keep a dishtowel close to the sink. Keep an extra towel or some paper towels handy to swiftly mop up any spills as you go.

Get the necessary equipment out. By doing this, you won't have to stop and seek for ingredients as you prepare your meal. Put a wet paper towel or nonstick pad underneath a cutting board if you plan to use one. As you work, this will prevent it from moving. With each dish in this book, you'll discover a list of the necessary tools and supplies. A cutting board and a chef's knife should always be brought out, along with some of the other necessities. It is usually a good idea to have them on hand because it is likely that you will need them.

All of the ingredients should be gathered, prepared, and placed in an accessible location. Just make sure that they are accessible if they need to be kept frozen or in a refrigerator.

Cooking Terminology

The language of cooking is distinct. When you are unclear about something in a recipe, you can consult this guide to cooking terminology for clarification, or you can even use it to test your knowledge.

To "beat" anything means to quickly mix it by hand or with an electric mixer in order to include air and make the mixture smooth.

To blend means to thoroughly integrate a number of individual materials.

To boil means to cook in liquid that is already boiling.

To chop something means to cut it into pieces with a knife.

To cream is to use the back of a spoon or an electric mixer to knead butter or shortening until it becomes light and fluffy. Sometimes, sugar is also added to the butter or shortening.

To lightly coat with flour or breadcrumbs. Also known as "dredge."

To grease means to coat the internal surface of a baking pan or dish with butter or another fat in order to prevent food from adhering to the pan while it is cooking. Greasing can also refer to the act of greasing.

Before placing food in the oven to cook, it is best to let the oven to come up to the desired temperature and "preheat."

To cook in liquid at a temperature slightly below the boiling point is to "simmer." Near a lower temperature than full boil, bubbles will continue to break at the surface, but at a considerably slower rate.

Heat settings: When you see "medium-low," "medium," and "medium-high" in a recipe, keep in mind that stoves have different settings and that it's best to think of the heat as it would cook butter:

Medium indicates that the butter will color rapidly, melt rapidly, and bubble strongly.

When the temperature is high, butter will bubble furiously, melt at an alarming rate, and turn brown in a matter of seconds.

How to Read a Recipe

Reading a recipe slowly and completely will help you achieve success. It is important that you read the recipe in its entirety before beginning the cooking process. Look up a word, method, technique, or substance that you are unfamiliar with if you don't know what it is. After that, you should reread the recipe in order to ensure that you fully comprehend the instructions.

When you have finished reading the recipe at least twice, you may get started on gathering, preparing, and measuring out the ingredients by taking out your tools.

1. The name of the dish 2. The amount of time, in minutes, that must be spent on the preparation of the recipe
2. Cook time, or the approximately required amount of time to prepare the recipe
3. A brief introduction to the cooking method in the headnote
4. The amount that will be produced by the dish or the number of people it will feed
5. A list of the components, in the order in which they are called for in the recipe, is referred to as the ingredient list.
6. Instructions: a detailed rundown of each and every step required to complete the dish.

When you create a recipe for the first time, you should make sure to follow the directions to the letter. Even a relatively minor alteration to the procedure can result in unsatisfactory output. After you have successfully completed a dish, you are free to experiment with the various seasonings and ingredients that have an effect on the flavor. Nevertheless, when you are baking, you should never change the amount of butter, flour, baking powder, or liquid in the recipe.

Measuring Skills

When it comes to cooking, having accurate measurements is essential to your success. Cooking is a science, and the only way to guarantee consistent results is to follow the measurements exactly as they are written in the recipe.

Dry ingredients

Measuring cups or measuring spoons are often used in order to accurately measure dry materials. Always use the flat edge of a kitchen knife to level off the top before measuring to ensure the most accurate results. The outcome of your recipe may change if you use a measuring cup that is either overfilled or underfilled with the components.

Be mindful that flour gains weight as it rests, as this will affect your measurements. After sifting the flour into the measuring cup, you should level it off without tapping the cup in order to obtain the most precise readings possible. If you do either of these things, you will end up with an erroneous measurement. Never tap the measuring cup as you fill it, and never dip the cup into the flour.

Liquids

If you want accurate results while measuring liquids, the best tool to use is a cup that is see-through, has graduated markings, and a spout for simple pouring. Placing the measuring cup on a surface that is level and then filling it precisely to the level that is wanted will result in an accurate measurement of the liquid being measured. In order to correctly read the measurement, you will need to stoop down so that the lines are at eye level.

When using the same cups or measuring spoons for dry and wet components, you'll want to measure the dry ingredients first, then the oils, and then the liquids like water. This will ensure that you get the best results possible.

Mixing Skills

The majority of recipes will instruct you to combine the wet and dry components in two separate bowls. It's an important step on the path to your achievement. When you combine the dry ingredients on their own, you ensure that the sugar, spices, and leavening agents are distributed uniformly throughout the mixture. This ensures that no single cookie will have all of the salt.

You will achieve better results, as well as a more equal texture and flavor in your finished product, if you use the method of combining wet ingredients separately from dry ingredients.

There are a variety of terms that are used to describe the process of combining diverse components. These are some of the terminologies that you'll find used in the recipes in this book, as well as in other cookbooks' recipes.

Stir

The majority of recipes call for separate mixing of the wet and dry ingredients. You must complete it if you want to succeed. The spices, sugar, and raising agents are evenly distributed when the dry ingredients are combined on their own. By doing this, the salt isn't consumed by just one cookie.

You will get better results and a finished product with a more uniform texture and consistent flavor if you use the technique of mixing wet ingredients and dry ingredients separately.

The process of combining materials is described using a variety of terminology. The following terms are used in this book's recipes as well as those in other cookbooks.

Fold

Typically, whipped cream or beaten egg whites are the subject of this activity. It is important to avoid letting the air that has been beaten into the whipped cream or egg whites escape when mixing them with heavier ingredients, like batter. A spoon is used to bring some of the combinations to the top by passing it through the bottom of the mixture and across the bottom. until mixed, repeat.

Toss

You employ a modest lift and drop technique when you "toss." You combine after turning the food over. Lift the lettuce and gently flip it over to coat all sides of the lettuce while "tossing" a salad.

Knife Skills

Safety with a knife comes down to proper grip. You'll be able to chop your food more precisely and consistently as well as give it a more polished appearance if you learn how to hold a knife.

How to Hold A Knife

The handle and the blade are the two main components of a knife. The bolster is the area where the handle and blade connect. The edge of a blade is its pointy portion.

Keep your hand behind the bolster and far from the edge when you are holding the knife. Wrap your fingers around the knife handle with your dominant hand. The knife handle should be covered by your thumb. You should be able to hold the knife handle comfortably.

Make sure the cutting board and the food are both stable before beginning to cut.

Slice

To slice is to cut thin pieces or strips of vegetables, fruits, meats, or bread. Meats should be sliced across the grain to keep the meat tender. When cutting vegetables, keep them stable on the cutting board by cutting them in half or cutting off a small section and placing the flat surface against the cutting board. As you are slicing, keep the blade in constant contact with your cutting board.

To slice a tomato: (1) Hold the tomato firmly with your non-knife hand. Using a paring knife, insert the tip ¼-inch near the core and rotate your knife around the stem. (2) Put the knife down and pull out the stem. Place the tomato, stem-side down, on the cutting board. Using your non-knife hand, curl your fingers under to hold the tomato in place and keep them away from the knife. Starting on one side and working across the tomato, use a chef's knife to cut ½-inch vertical slices.

Rough chop

A rough chop is a way to cut larger chunks (about ½-inch to 1-inch square). A rough chop is larger and less exact than dice or mince.

To chop an apple: (1) Using a vegetable peeler, remove the skin, if desired. Slice off the bottom of the apple so it rests flat on the cutting board. Cut the apple in half lengthwise. Cut a "V" around the core lengthwise and remove it. Lay the flat interior side of the apple against the cutting board. Using your non-knife hand, curl your fingers under to hold the apple and cut it into about ½-inch vertical slices. (2) On the broadside, cut the slices in half lengthwise. They should now look like wide "sticks." Turn the "sticks" 90° and chop them into roughly ½-inch cubes.

Dice

To dice is to cut the food into small, uniform cubes.

To dice an onion: (1) Using a chef's knife, cut the top of the onion off and discard. Place the flat, cut side down, on a cutting board, and cut the onion in half. Peel the onion. Then, place one of the halves, cut side down again, on the cutting board. Stopping just short of the root end (leave it intact to keep the onion together), cut ¼-inch vertical slices. (2) Turn the onion 90° and cut into the onion horizontally (your knife will be parallel to the cutting board) in ¼-inch increments. (Again, keep the root end intact.) Then, starting from the top and working your way to the root end, slice the onion crosswise in ¼-inch increments. As you do this, ¼-inch cubes will fall from the onion and accumulate at the cut end. Repeat with the other half.

Mince

To mince means to cut into very small pieces (⅛-inch square or smaller).

To mince a clove of garlic: (1) Cut off the root end. Put the garlic clove on the cutting board. Place the blade of a chef's knife flat against the clove with the edge facing away from you. With your palm flat against the knife blade and your fingers up, press down on the blade to gently crush the clove. (2) Remove the papery skin. Roughly chop the garlic clove. Turn the blade to a normal cutting position and place your non-knife hand on top of the knife blade, keeping your fingers and thumb up. Rock the blade back and forth, up and down, cutting the garlic into fine pieces. Use the knife blade to scrape the garlic into a pile and repeat until the garlic is very small and almost a paste-like consistency.

Other Cuts

One of the most versatile pieces of equipment in your kitchen is a box grater. It offers four sides that help you cut small pieces of food in a variety of ways.

Grate

To cut food into small strips using the large holes on a box grater. Common foods that you might grate include cheese, carrots, or zucchini. You might also grate apples for oatmeal using this side of the grater.

Shred

To tear or cut into thin pieces or strips. For meat, you can do this with two forks, two knives, or sometimes with an electric mixer. Shred cooked chicken breasts. For vegetables or cheeses, use the medium-size holes on a box grater.

Zest

To cut small shavings or particles, usually of the outer skin of citrus fruits. You can use a handheld zester or the smallest set of holes on a box grater.

Peel

To remove the outer covering of something like a banana, or other fruit or vegetables. This can be done by hand or with a tool depending on what you are peeling. Tools you can use include a paring knife, a vegetable peeler, or the smile-shaped slicing blades on the side of a box grater.

Cooking in a Pan

These three cooking processes are closely related, are all relatively quick, and use medium-high to high heat, but the amount of oil or fat that you use varies.

Sauté

Sautéing is when you use a small amount of oil and high heat to quickly cook food. The fast cooking keeps the flavors sharp. Warm the pan over medium-high heat, add minimal fat, and then add the food you are sautéing. Stir frequently.

Fry

Frying is cooking food in hot oil. To fry, you will heat the oil in the pan over medium-high to high heat, then when it reaches the desired temperature, place the food in the oil to cook.

The difference between frying and sautéing is that sautéing uses direct heat, while frying is done by immersing the food in the hot oil.

Sear

Searing browns, the surface of meats, quickly creating a crust that seals in moisture. It can be done in a skillet or on a grill. This method uses very little oil and is done at high heat for a short time.

Cooking in an Oven

Methods of cooking in the oven are differentiated primarily by heat source and temperature.

Bake

To cook in the dry heat in an oven. It usually is done at lower temperatures—up to 375°F. Baking usually involves foods that start as a batter or dough.

Roast

To cook food in an uncovered pan in the dry heat of an oven at a temperature of at least 400°F. Roasting usually involves foods that have structure, like meats and vegetables.

Broil

To cook under the direct, top-down heat of a broiler. This method differs from baking and roasting since the food is turned during the process and cooks only on one side at a time, rather than on all sides evenly.

Essential Tools

Cooking is easier and faster with the right equipment. Look around your kitchen. Some—or all—of the items that you'll need may already be in your drawers and cupboards, including:

Knives. A chef's knife is the primary knife you will use in the kitchen. It is about 8 inches long and 1½ inches wide. It can be used to slice, chop, dice, and mince. Also, consider a paring knife (a small knife for peeling and coring fruits and vegetables) and a serrated knife (a scallop-edged knife for cutting bread).

CAUTION! Nothing is worse than a dull knife! Contrary to popular belief, a dull knife is more dangerous than a sharp one. A dull blade rips and tears because it requires more pressure to do the job. The added pressure also increases the chance of slippage. For safety and efficiency, use sharp knives.

Cutting boards. You'll need two separate cutting boards, one for meat, poultry, and seafood, and another for everything else. Wood, bamboo, or plastic cutting boards are best for your knives.

Measuring cups. Look for a set of measuring cups that includes the ¼ cup, ⅓ cup, ½ cup, and 1 cup sizes for dry ingredients and a large glass measuring cup for liquids.

Measuring spoons. Measuring spoons are used to measure smaller amounts of dry or liquid ingredients.

Mixing bowls. Mixing bowls are your go-to for mixing marinades, sauces, batters, and more. A set of three—one small, one medium, and one large—will get you started.

Colander. A colander is a great tool for draining pasta, washing vegetables, and draining canned ingredients.

Whisk. One of the most used items in my kitchen, a whisk can be used to make salad dressings and sauces, beat eggs, and combine wet or dry ingredients.

Box grater. A grater is a multipurpose tool. It serves as a grater and a zester.

Skillet. You'll need a skillet for sautéing and frying. A 10-inch skillet will get you started.

Saucepan. Saucepans are for cooking soups, pasta, and sauces. A small (1½ quart) and medium saucepan (4 quarts) are good starters.

Large pot. A 6-quart pot is ideal for the larger soup, stew, and pasta recipes.

Baking sheet. Indispensable for baking cookies, baking sheets are also great for roasting vegetables or making nachos for a crowd. Look for a jelly roll pan, or a baking sheet with a lip, which is more versatile and prevents overflow.

Muffin pan. Choose one with either 6 or 12 built-in muffin cups.

Baking pan. This is a large, deep dish with high edges that is oven-proof. The most common sizes and shapes are an 8-by-8-inch square or a 9-by-13-inch rectangle.

Rubber spatula. This is a wide flexible cooking tool used for scraping wet ingredients out of a bowl or pan, as well as mixing and folding.

Turner spatula. This is a tool with a hard, wide, flat end used for flipping eggs, pancakes, French toast, hamburgers, etc.

Cooking spoons. Look for a small assortment of cooking spoons, including a wooden spoon, stirring spoon, slotted spoon, and ladle, which are all very helpful in the kitchen.

Tongs. These are used to grip and lift objects instead of holding them directly with your hands.

Oven mitts. These protect your hands and forearms when taking hot items out of the oven.

Digital cooking thermometer. This will help ensure food is cooked to the proper temperature.

Blender. A traditional blender or an immersion blender will help you make smoothies, sauces, and soups.

Microwave Hacks

Microwaves do so much more than just heating leftovers. I remember when my family got our first microwave and my mother cooked our entire Thanksgiving dinner, including the turkey, in the microwave.

Cooking things like bacon, baked potatoes, and dried beans are known for being easier and quicker in the microwave. But did you know that zapping a lemon for 20 seconds makes it easier to juice? Or that you can microwave cake frosting for about 30 seconds (or until a uniformly thin consistency) and pour it over a cake for a perfectly smooth frosting?

You can even use the microwave for cleanup. Sanitize your scrubby kitchen sponges by saturating them with water and microwaving for 1 minute or disinfect small wooden cutting boards by putting them in the microwave for 30 seconds to 1 minute.

Safety First

Whether you're a novice cook or an experienced chef, kitchen safety is a priority, and safety starts with prevention. Review the following safety precautions before getting started in the kitchen.

<u>Fires</u>

To prevent kitchen fires, take the following precautions:

- Keep a fire extinguisher near the stove.

- Make sure the smoke alarms in your home are in working order.

- Familiarize yourself with what to do in case of a fire.

- Do not leave anything you are cooking on the stove unattended.

- Do not put metal of any kind (metal bowls, silverware, aluminum foil, etc.) into the microwave.

- If a fire should break out, act quickly, and respond appropriately:

- *Fire in a cooking pan on the stove.* Do NOT move the pan. Wearing an oven mitt, place a lid on the pan to smother the flames. Turn off the stove. If you cannot safely put the lid on the pan, use a fire extinguisher, targeting the base of the fire.

- *Grease fire.* Do NOT use water! Instead, throw baking soda or salt on the flames, or use a fire extinguisher.

- *Fire in the oven or microwave.* Leave the door closed to suffocate the flames. Turn the appliance off immediately.

- If the fire is spreading and you can't control it, get everyone out of the house and call 911.

Burns

Burns occur when hot water, hot oil, steam, or hot metal come in contact with the skin. To prevent burns:

- Turn pan handles away from other burners and away from the edge of the stove.
- Wear an apron, tie your hair back, and do not wear long loose sleeves while cooking.
- Keep oven mitts near the stove.
- Never touch the stovetop or an oven rack with your bare hands.
- Stand back when cooking with hot water, hot oil, and other hot liquids.

Bacteria

Bacteria are invisible but can cause mild to severe illness. To avoid bacterial infection, be sure to:

- Always wash your hands before you start cooking and frequently throughout the cooking process, and after handling any raw meat, fish, or uncooked eggs.
- Keep raw meat, eggs, fish, and dairy refrigerated when not in use.
- Refrigerate anything with meat, fish, eggs, and dairy within two hours of cooking.
- Wash your cutting boards after each use.
- Cook meat to the recommended internal temperature.
- Do not put food on a plate that has had raw meat on it.
- Do not eat raw eggs or batters with raw eggs.

Cuts

Most cuts in the kitchen are caused by knives, so let's talk about knife safety:

- Always cut away from your body.

- Don't lick knives.

- Don't use a knife to pry open canned goods.

- Never drop a knife into a sink of dishwater. Instead, wash it immediately and put it away.

10 Ways to Be a Better Cook

- Gain wisdom from your past errors: There will be unsuccessful attempts at your recipes. Nothing to worry about. Sometimes it's just a bad day, and sometimes it's a learning opportunity.

- My daughters refer to this as my "company cooking" because despite the fact that I can make the same food 100 times without issue, when I have people around for dinner, the same recipe is a complete and utter failure.

- When a recipe doesn't turn out the way you hoped it would, it's natural to feel a sense of disappointment. Do not allow yourself to become disheartened, and do not give up. Have fun on the trip and keep working in the kitchen.

- Read the recipe several times over: Read through the recipe in its entirety to get a sense of the steps involved and the materials required. Check that you have all of the necessary ingredients and reread the recipe to see if there are any terms pertaining to cooking that you need to seek up. Every time I add a new component to the dish, I go back through the recipe and read it all the way through to ensure that I am adding the exact quantity and that I am not missing any steps or components. Because this is of such vital significance, I will state it once again.

- Keep to the instructions: When I first cook a dish using a new recipe, I never deviate from the instructions in any manner. Then, I pay attention to what those who are eating it have to say, and I make a mental note of it so that the next time I make the recipe, I may modify it to better suit the preferences of the people whose stomachs I'm filling.

- For instance, some individuals find the flavor of cilantro to be unpleasant. If you are aware of this fact and are preparing salsa, you could want to experiment with fresh basil, oregano, or parsley, or perhaps a combination of these three.

- Ask for assistance: Even though I'm an adult, I still give my mom a call whenever I have a question about cooking. She has been cooking for a longer period of time than I have, and as a result, she has a lot of information to share. Asking someone for a recipe can also help you comprehend why you're doing certain things, such as separating the dry components from the wet elements so that they mix more evenly or bringing something up to a certain temperature (to reduce, solidify, or change the structure).

- Always use high-quality components: The final flavor of your food will be heavily influenced by the components you use, so be sure they are of good quality. Always use the greatest ingredients you can get your hands on, and whenever it's possible, try to utilize fresh ingredients. But don't assume that more expensive means better when it comes to the ingredients. You can find exceptional pieces of meat at prices that work with your budget by going to a local butcher or shopping at a farmer's market for fresh products.

- To suit one's palate: Follow the recipe exactly as it is written, and as you go along, taste what you're making and adjust the seasonings accordingly. You want all of the flavors to meld together so that none of the seasonings take precedence over the others.

- Maintain a tidy workspace by giving yourself brief intervals during the preparation of the recipe to tidy up your work area. When you are done, throw away the skins of the vegetables, put the ingredients away as you use them, and clean up any spills as soon as they occur. To make the most of the time while the food is simmering or otherwise being prepared, you should clean the dishes. You'll have more time to savor the meal you've prepared and less time to devote to cleaning up the colossal mess that will inevitably follow it.

- Cook like a pro: You put in a lot of effort to create something delicious, so you should make sure to display it in the best possible way by plating it. If you imagine the surface of the plate to be the dial of a clock, you can arrange the portions of protein, starch, and vegetables so that they correspond to the hours two, six, and ten, respectively. Additionally, the use of odd numbers (for example, placing three or five shrimp on a plate rather than two or four) creates the illusion that there is more food on the plate. If you want to add some color to the dish, you can always use an edible garnish such as sprigs of parsley, sprinkles of fresh herbs, or slices of fresh fruit.

- Experiment with different things: Keep an open mind when it comes to trying new foods. Try a little bit of something that you've never had before. Test your sense of smell and taste to see if you can recognize different spices and foods. Examine the texture of the dish. Is it thick or light in texture? Is the sauce on the thicker or more runny side? What else do you notice with your eyes, nose, and tongue? By venturing outside of your comfort zone, you may discover a new seasoning or herb, as well as the kind of foods that go well with it. If you try something and don't like it the first time, try it again with a different seasoning or preparation.

- Hone your skills in creating your distinctive dish: Find a meal that you enjoy making in the kitchen and make that dish your signature dish. Make it a point to hone your skills, solicit input from others, and take satisfaction in the finished product.

Recipe reality

Cooking allows for some degree of flexibility, and an accomplished cook is able to alter and adapt to changing circumstances in the kitchen. The more you cook, the better you'll be able to adjust recipes to suit your personal preferences, even when following them exactly. Everyone has their own unique taste preferences. There are those that enjoy their cuisine with a greater amount of heat, while others could favor a dish with less intensity.

If a recipe doesn't work out as planned, look at the experience as a chance to improve your cooking skills and give it another shot, this time making a mental note of any adjustments that might improve the outcome. When following a recipe, if it feels like something is missing from the dish, you may always add an item that will hopefully make it taste better to you. In many of my recipes, I've given tips and tricks for experimenting with a wide variety of items that can be substituted in their place. Feel free to make adjustments to the recipes in this book so that they better suit your preferences as you gain more knowledge about the components that contribute to flavor and how to create it.

Breakfast

1. Hard-Boiled Eggs

- Prep: 15 Minutes
- Serve: 2

Ingredients:

- a total of four eggs, at room temperature
- Three glasses' worth of water

Directions:

1. Eggs should be placed in a medium pot, which should have one inch of water on top of the eggs.
2. Bring the water to a boil in the pot over high heat with the lid on.
3. The pot should then be immediately turned off the heat so that the egg can stand in water for 12 minutes.
4. After 12 minutes, remove the boiled eggs and put them in a sizable bowl with cold water.

5. Take the eggs out, let them to cool completely, and then peel the eggs.
6. As you please, serve the eggs.

Nutrition:

- Kcal: 310 Cal
- Carbs: 2.2 g
- Protein: 26 g

2. Herb and Cheese Omelet

- Prep: 5 Minutes
- Serve: 1

Ingredients:

- basil, minced into two tablespoons.
- Salt: 1/16 teaspoon; powdered pepper: 1/16 teaspoon
- 1 teaspoon unsalted butter
- At room temperature, three eggs
- 2 tablespoons of cheddar cheese, shredded.

Directions:

1. Chiffonade the basil leaves.
2. In a sizable bowl, crack the eggs, add the basil, salt, and black pepper, and whisk to mix.
3. Take a 6-inch wide, big skillet, turn the heat to low, add the butter, and wait for it to melt.
4. Pour the egg mixture into the pan while tilting it to evenly coat it with the melted butter. Next, whisk it with a rubber spatula right away.
5. The top of the eggs will be a little runny and the bottom will be cooked; continue pushing the outer portion of the cooked egg toward the center until the egg starts to firm up.

6. Add cheese to the omelet after it has been cooked for 1 to 2 minutes, or until the cheese melts.

7. With the use of a spatula, loosen the omelet's edge so you can slide it onto a plate and fold it.

Nutrition:

- Kcal: 256 Cal
- Carbs: 1 g
- Protein: 21 g

3. Eggs in the Hole

- Prep: 10 Minutes
- Serve: 1

Ingredients:

- Eight pieces of whole grain bread
- 4 bacon pieces, ¼ teaspoon salt
- ¼ teaspoon ground black pepper and 1 tablespoon unsalted butter
- At room temperature, four eggs

Directions:

1. A large skillet pan should be heated for three minutes over medium-high heat.

2. Add the bacon, and cook it for 3 to 4 minutes on each side, or until it is crisp and golden.

3. Once the platter is ready and covered with paper towels, arrange the bacon slices on it with a pair of tongs and set them aside until needed.

4. Prepare the bread by using any 2 12-inch cookie cutter, such as a circle, heart, or star, and cutting a piece from the middle of each slice of bread.

5. Brush this mixture on bread slices and cutout pieces after melting the butter in the pan.

6. Put two slices with cutouts into the pan and cook for 1 minute on each side, or until beautifully browned.

7. Each hole on the bread slice should have an egg in it. Cook for two minutes, then carefully flip the slice over and cut it into pieces.

8. Add 1/16 teaspoons of salt and black pepper to each egg, then cook the eggs for a further 2 minutes, or until the yolks are runny.

9. Repeat with the remaining eggs and bread pieces after transferring the eggs in the holes to the plates.

Nutrition:

- Kcal: 320 Cal
- Carbs: 12 g
- Protein: 15 g

4. Egg Salad Sandwiches

- Prep: 10 Minutes
- Serve: 6

Ingredients:

- 12 hard-boiled, peeled eggs
- 2 chopped green onions.
- Whole-wheat bread in 12 pieces
- 4 grains of salt
- ¼ teaspoon of black pepper, ground
- 4 tablespoons of unsalted butter
- ½ cup of mayonnaise

Directions:

1. Put the butter in a microwave-safe bowl, and heat it for 15 seconds to soften it.

2. Follow the hard-boiled egg recipe's instructions for boiling the eggs.

3. Boiling eggs should be placed in a bowl of cold water, rested for ten minutes, and then peeled.

4. The eggs should be divided into slices and then forked.

5. Stir in the mayonnaise, green onion, salt, and pepper once you've added them all.

6. Spread two slices of bread with two and a third tablespoons of butter before assembling the first sandwich.

7. Cover the buttered side of one slice of bread with 2 to 3 tablespoons of the egg mixture, and then top with the second slice of bread.

8. Serve the remaining sandwiches after assembling them similarly.

Nutrition:

- Kcal: 244 Cal
- Carbs: 14.5 g
- Protein: 9 g

5. Grilled Cheese Sandwich

- Prep: 10 Minutes
- Serve: 1

Ingredients:

- 4 cheddar cheese slices
- 8 tablespoons of unsalted butter
- Eight pieces of wheat bread

Directions:

1. Put the butter in a microwave-safe bowl, and heat it for 15 seconds to soften it.

2. Each piece of bread should have 12 tbsp butter spread on one side.

3. A large skillet pan should be heated for two minutes at medium heat.

4. Next, insert a slice of butter-side-down bread in it, top it with a slice of cheese, and cover it with a third slice of butter-side-up bread.

5. Place a small, flat-bottomed, heavy pot on top of the cheese sandwich that is in the pan. The pot should be slightly larger than the sandwich.

6. The bottom side of the pot should have gone brown by the time it is taken out of the sandwich after three minutes.

7. Remove the cheese sandwich from the pan, top it with 1 tablespoon of butter, and then flip it over.

8. Place the pot back over the sandwich and cook it for a further three minutes.

9. The sandwich's opposite side should be golden and the cheese should have melted after 3 minutes.

10. Repeat with the remaining sandwiches after transferring the cooked sandwich to a platter.

11. Serve each sandwich after cutting it in half when it's time to eat.

Nutrition:

- Kcal: 262 Cal
- Carbs: 25 g
- Protein: 13 g

6. Egg Wraps

- Prep: 5 Minutes
- Serve: 2

Ingredients:

- Four pieces of ham
- 1 cup fresh spinach leaves
- 1 small avocado
- At room temperature, four eggs

- Olive oil, 1 tbsp
- water in 2 tablespoons
- 4 cheddar cheese slices

Extra Ingredients:

- 1/4 teaspoon each of salt and black pepper

Directions:

1. Remove the avocado's pit, scoop out the flesh, and then slice the flesh after cutting the avocado in half lengthwise.
2. In a medium bowl, crack the eggs, season with salt and pepper, and whisk to mix.
3. A medium skillet pan should be used, which should be heated to a hot temperature over medium-high heat with oil added.
4. Pour half of the egg mixture into the pan, turn it to cover the entire surface, and cook for 2 minutes or until it becomes hard.
5. Transferring the omelet to a cutting board comes after flipping the egg and cooking it for 1 minute.
6. Make another omelet with the remaining egg mixture by repeating the process.
7. Create the wrap by layering one omelet with two pieces of cheese in the center, followed by two slices of ham, a half cup of spinach, and a half of avocado.
8. With the leftover omelet, cheese, ham, spinach, and avocado, make another wrap after rolling the egg over the filling.

Nutrition:

- Kcal: 284 Cal
- Carbs: 25.5 g
- Protein: 12 g

- Prep: 10 Minutes
- Serve: 15 sticks

Ingredients:

- bread, five slices of whole wheat
- ½ teaspoon of cinnamon powder
- 2 teaspoons honey and 1/8 teaspoon salt
- at room temperature, two eggs
- 1 tablespoon unsalted butter and 2 cups whole milk

Directions:

1. To make the breadsticks, trim the bread slices' edges with a serrated knife before cutting them into 1-inch sticks.
2. In a medium bowl, crack the eggs, add the salt, honey, and cinnamon, then pour in the milk and whisk to incorporate.
3. Take a breadstick, coat it well in the egg mixture, and then set it on a platter.
4. Repeat the process with the remaining breadsticks.
5. Place the butter in a medium skillet over medium heat and allow it to melt.
6. Breadsticks should be added to the pan until it is full, and then they should be cooked for 3 minutes on each side or until golden brown.
7. Repeat with the remaining breadsticks after transferring the completed ones to a platter using a tong.

Nutrition:

- Kcal: 360 Cal
- Carbs: 52.5 g
- Protein: 6 g

- Prep: 10 Minutes
- Serve: 2

Ingredients:

- 4 bacon slices
- 2 English muffins made with whole wheat.
- 4 cheese slices ¼ teaspoon salt ¼ teaspoon black pepper
- 2 tablespoons of unsalted butter
- At room temperature, four eggs

Directions:

1. A frying pan should be heated for two minutes on medium heat.
2. Place the bacon slices in the pan and cook for 2 to 3 minutes on each side, or until crisp and brown.
3. Once finished, move the bacon slices to a platter covered in paper towels.
4. Toast each muffin after cutting it in half lengthwise.
5. Toast the muffins and butter each half with a half a teaspoon of butter.
6. Put the muffins' bottom halves on a plate. After that, add two slices of cheese and two slices of bacon to each muffin.
7. The remaining butter should be added to a big frying pan and melted over medium heat.
8. Crack the eggs into the pan, season with salt and pepper, and cook for 3 to 4 minutes, or until the whites are set.
9. After gently turning the eggs, heat for another two minutes.
10. After placing two eggs on top of the bacon layer, top the muffin with the remaining halves, and serve.

Nutrition:

- Kcal: 520 Cal

- Carbs: 37 g
- Protein: 26 g

9. Quinoa, Cranberry, and Almond Granola

- Prep: 10 Minutes
- Serve: 12

Ingredients:

- Old-fashioned rolled oats, 4 cups.
- 2 cups of uncooked quinoa and 1 cup of sweetened dried cranberries.
- 2 cups of sweetened coconut shreds
- Almonds, chopped, 1 ½ cups
- ½ cup unsalted, roasted sunflower seeds 2 ½ tablespoons unsweetened vanilla extract

Extra Ingredients:

- 1 teaspoon of cinnamon powder
- Brown sugar, 1 cup.
- 1 teaspoon of nutmeg, ground
- Olive oil, 1/3 cup.
- water, 1/3 cup.

Directions:

1. Turn on the oven, then lower the temperature to 350°F and let it warm up.
2. Brown sugar and water should be added to a small saucepan in the meanwhile.
3. Place the pan over medium-high heat, stir occasionally, and cook for 3 minutes, or until the sugar is completely dissolved and the mixture is boiling.
4. In a sizable bowl, combine the oats with the coconut, quinoa, almonds, sunflower seeds, salt, nutmeg, and cinnamon. Stir to combine.

5. Pour the syrup over the quinoa-oat mixture after whisking in the vanilla and oil after the sugar mixture has reached a boil.
6. The oat mixture and syrup should be well mixed using a rubber spatula.
7. Spoon the oat mixture onto a baking sheet, and then use the back of a spoon to push it into an equal layer.
8. Bake the oats for 45 minutes, tossing them every ten minutes, until they are golden brown. Place the baking sheet in the oven.
9. When ready, take the baking sheet out of the oven and stir the oat mixture occasionally while it cools fully.
10. When the granola has cooled, stir in the cranberries. Store it in an airtight jar until needed.
11. Eat it right away or pair it with yogurt when it's ready to eat.

Nutrition:

- Kcal: 583 Cal
- Carbs: 76 g
- Protein: 11 g

- Prep: 5 Minutes
- Serve: 1

Ingredients:

- spinach, 1 cup.
- 2 tablespoons of white onion, chopped.
- 1 chopped green chile, ¼ teaspoon cumin seeds.
- 2 eggs, at room temperature, and 2 teaspoons unsalted butter
- 8 grains of salt
- 1/8 teaspoon of black pepper, ground

Directions:

1. In a bowl, crack the eggs, then whisk them until they are foamy.
2. One teaspoon of butter should be added to a frying pan over medium heat before the cumin seeds are added.

3. When the cumin seeds begin to crackle, add the green pepper, onion, and simmer for an additional 3 to 5 minutes, or until the veggies are golden brown.
4. Add the chopped spinach, cook for 3 minutes, or until the spinach becomes green, and then turn off the heat.
5. Add salt to the bowl containing the eggs, then whisk until the spinach mixture is thoroughly combined.
6. Melt the remaining butter in the frying pan over low heat once again.
7. Black pepper should be sprinkled over the egg before the omelet is cooked for 4 minutes, or until the bottom is set. Pour the spinach-egg mixture onto the pan and spread it out evenly.
8. The omelet should be carefully flipped, cooked for an additional two minutes, and then moved to a plate.

Nutrition:

- Kcal: 236 Cal
- Carbs: 3.7 g
- Protein: 16 g

11. Yogurt with Cereal and Bananas

- Prep: 10 Minutes
- Serve: 4

Ingredients:

- 4 small bananas
- 2 cups of cereal Cheerios
- Greek yogurt, one cup

Directions:

1. Slice the bananas once they have been peeled.

2. Take four mason jars or glass dishes, and layer 1/4 cup of yogurt on the bottom of each.

3. In each jar, place a layer of cereal and banana slices on top of the yogurt layer.

4. Serve after adding the last of the yogurt on top, followed by the last of the cereal and banana slices.

Nutrition:

- Kcal: 196 Cal
- Carbs: 42 g
- Protein: 6 g

12. Whole-Wheat Waffles

- Prep: 10 Minutes
- Serve: 8

Ingredients:

- Whole-wheat flour, 1 ½ tablespoons
- 1 teaspoon unsweetened vanilla extract
- 1/3 cup unsalted butter
- maple syrup, two tablespoons
- 12 ounces of whole milk
- At ambient temperature, one egg
- Baking powder, two teaspoons
- 4 grains of salt

Directions:

1. Turn the waffle maker on, then wait for it to heat up.

2. Butter should be melted fully after being placed in a medium heatproof bowl and being microwaved for one minute or more.

3. Whisk the eggs, vanilla, and maple syrup into the melted butter until well incorporated.

4. Add the flour, salt, and baking powder to a separate medium bowl and whisk to incorporate.

5. There shouldn't be any lumps in the batter. Add 12 cup of the flour combination to the egg mixture and whisk until combined. Add the remaining flour, 12 cup at a time, and whisk until combined.

6. Pour 12 cup of the batter into the waffle iron that has been heated, cover it with the lid, and cook for 5 to 7 minutes, or until the batter is firm and golden brown.

7. Repeat with the remaining batter after transferring the cooked waffles to a plate with a tong.

8. Waffles should be served with honey and your favorite sliced fruits.

Nutrition:

- Kcal: 305 Cal
- Carbs: 37 g
- Protein: 11 g

13. Chocolate and Avocado Smoothie

- Prep: 5 Minutes
- Serve: 4

Ingredients:

- Frozen bananas, two
- 1 small avocado
- Flax seeds, 2 tablespoons
- Cocoa powder, 6 teaspoons
- Honey, two tablespoons
- two mugs of whole milk

Directions:

1. Bananas should be peeled, cut into slices, and then added to a food processor.
2. Remove the avocado's pit, cut it in half, and add the flesh to a food processor.
3. Add the other ingredients, close the top, and pulse until smooth for 30 seconds.
4. Serve the smoothie after dividing it equally among four glasses.

Nutrition:

- Kcal: 339.3 Cal
- Carbs: 44.3 g
- Protein: 17.2 g

14. Flaxseed and Blueberry Oatmeal

- Prep: 5 Minutes
- Serve: 2

Ingredients:

- 1 cup of old-fashioned rolled oats.
- 1/3 cup fresh blueberries
- 2 teaspoons of flaxseed, ground
- 2 tablespoons of toasted, chopped pecans.
- 1 glass of whole milk
- ¾ cup water
- Salt, 1/16 teaspoon
- 1 teaspoon of honey

Directions:

1. Place a small pot over medium heat, add the milk, and then bring it to a boil.
2. Then immediately reduce the heat to medium-low, toss in the salt, oats, and flax seeds, and stir until well combined.

3. Stirring constantly, cook the oatmeal for 7 minutes or until the oats are soft, and then turn off the heat.

4. Oats should be thoroughly stirred, allowed to cool for two minutes, then divided equally between two bowls. The pan should be covered.

5. Each bowl of oatmeal should have 1 tablespoon pecans, 3 tablespoons of berries, and 12 tablespoon honey on top before being served.

Nutrition:

- Kcal: 340 Cal
- Carbs: 49.2 g
- Protein: 11.9 g

15. Flaxseed and Raisin Bread

- Prep: 10 Minutes
- Serve: 1 bread

Ingredients:

- Whole-wheat flour, 1 cup
- sugar, 1/3 cup
- ¾ cup flaxseed and 1 cup rolled oats
- 100 g raisins
- 1 glass of whole milk
- 1 cup piping hot water.
- one tablespoon of baking soda
- ¼ teaspoon salt and 1 teaspoon baking powder

Directions:

1. Turn on the oven, lower the temperature to 350 degrees, and let it warm up.

2. In the meantime, oil a loaf pan that measures 9 by 5 inches.

3. In a sizable bowl, add the raisins, then add the boiling water, stir in the baking soda, and let the raisins sit for five minutes.
4. When just combined, add the oats, whole-wheat flour, salt, sugar, and baking powder. Spoon the batter into the prepared loaf pan.
5. Bake the bread for one hour and fifteen minutes, or until the top is very brown, in the loaf pan.
6. When done, remove the bread from the pan and allow it cool entirely on a wire rack after 10 minutes.
7. Slice the chilled bread into sixteen pieces before serving.

Nutrition:

- Kcal: 260 Cal
- Carbs: 46 g
- Protein: 4 g

16. Healthy Buckwheat Porridge

- Prep: 10 minutes
- Serve: 2

Ingredients:

- 1 cup of rinsed buckwheat grout
- 1 teaspoon of cinnamon powder
- 3 cups of unsweetened almond milk, 1 sliced banana
- A dash of salt

Directions:

1. Cooking spray should be used inside the instant pot.
2. Stir well after adding each ingredient to the instant pot.
3. Cook for 6 minutes on high while covering the pot with a lid.
4. Once finished, use quick release to remove pressure. Open the lid.

Nutrition:

- Kcal: 316 Cal
- Carbs: 59.8 g
- Protein: 9.8 g

17. Apricot Oats

- Prep: 10 minutes
- Serve: 2

Ingredients:

- steel-cut oats, 1 cup.
- 1 cup chopped dried apricots and 1 ½ cups water.
- 1 ½ cups almond milk without sugar

Directions:

1. Cooking spray should be used inside the instant pot.
2. Stir well after adding each ingredient to the instant pot.
3. Cook for 3 minutes on high while covering the pot with a lid.
4. Once finished, use quick release to remove pressure. Open the lid.

Nutrition:

- Kcal: 222 Cal
- Carbs: 37.7 g
- Protein: 7.1 g

- Prep: 10 minutes
- Serve: 6

Ingredients:

- quinoa, 1 ½ cups, washed and drained.
- 1.5 cups of water
- ½ tsp. vanilla
- maple syrup, 2 tablespoons
- ¼ teaspoon of cinnamon, ground
- A dash of salt

Directions:

1. Cooking spray should be used inside the instant pot.
2. Stir well after adding each ingredient to the instant pot.
3. Cover the saucepan with a lid and heat it for one minute.
4. Once finished, allow pressure to drop naturally for 10 minutes before using a fast release to release the residual pressure. Open the lid.
5. With a fork, fluff quinoa before serving.

Nutrition:

- Kcal: 175 Cal
- Carbs: 31.9 g
- Protein: 6 g

- Prep: 10 minutes
- Serve: 2

Ingredients:

- steel-cut oats, 1 cup.
- maple syrup, 1 tbsp
- ¼ tsp. of cinnamon
- 10 raisins, 1 tbsp
- 1 tablespoon chopped dried apricots.
- 1 tablespoon of cranberries, dried
- apple juice, 1 cup.
- 3 glasses of water
- A dash of salt

Directions:

1. Cooking spray should be used inside the instant pot.
2. Stir well after adding each ingredient to the instant pot.
3. Cook for 5 minutes on high while covering the pot with a lid.
4. Once finished, allow pressure to drop naturally for 10 minutes before using a fast release to release the residual pressure. Open the lid.

Nutrition:

- Kcal: 256 Cal
- Carbs : 53.1 g
- Protein : 5.7 g

- Prep: 10 minutes
- Serve: 4

Ingredients:

- Rolling oats, 1 ½ cups
- 1 teaspoon of honey
- 2 diced apples
- 1 cup of almond milk without sugar
- 1.5 cups of water
- A dash of salt

Directions:

1. Cooking spray should be used inside the instant pot.
2. Stir well after adding each ingredient to the instant pot.
3. Put a lid on the pot, choose the slow cook setting, and simmer the food for three hours on low.

Nutrition:

- Kcal: 200 Cal
- Carbs: 41 g
- Protein: 4.6 g

21. Chocolate Quinoa Bowl

- Prep: 10 minutes
- Serve: 2

Ingredients:

- quinoa, 1 ½ cups, washed and drained
- ¼ tsp. of cinnamon
- ½ tsp. vanilla
- Unsweetened cocoa powder in a half-teaspoon
- maple syrup, 2 tablespoons
- 1 cup of almond milk without sugar
- ¾ cups of water
- A dash of salt

Directions:

1. Cooking spray should be used inside the instant pot.
2. Stir well after adding each ingredient to the instant pot.
3. Cover the saucepan with a lid and heat it for one minute.
4. Once finished, allow pressure to drop naturally for 10 minutes before using a fast release to release the residual pressure. Open the lid.
5. With a fork, fluff quinoa before serving.

Nutrition:

- Kcal: 549 Cal
- Carbs: 97.3 g

- Protein: 18.8 g

22. Coconut Strawberry Oatmeal

- Prep: 10 minutes
- Serve: 6

Ingredients:

- 1 cup freshly cut strawberries.
- Coconut flakes, 1 cup.
- 1 teaspoon of cinnamon powder
- ½ cup cream of coconut
- 2 cups of almond milk without sugar

Directions:

1. Cooking spray should be used inside the instant pot.
2. Stir well after adding each ingredient to the instant pot.
3. Cook for 10 minutes on high while covering the pot with a lid.
4. Once finished, use quick release to remove pressure. Open the lid.

Nutrition:

- Kcal: 115 Cal
- Carbs: 6 g
- Protein: 1.4 g

- Prep: 10 minutes
- Serve: 4

Ingredients:

- 8 eggs
- Breakfast sausage, 1 lb.
- ½ medium onion, chopped, and 4 ounces of cheddar cheese
- season to taste
- ½ tsp. dried parsley
- ½ tsp. paprika
- 1 teaspoon of powdered garlic
- 1 teaspoon of powdered onion

Directions:

1. To avoid sticking, heat the skillet over medium heat using butter or nonstick spray.
2. Sausage should be browned over medium-high heat while being broken up into tiny, even pieces using a spatula.
3. Diced onion should be added to the pan after the meat has mostly browned and cooked until transparent.
4. Mix the eggs, herbs, and spices thoroughly in a large basin.
5. Cheese should be added to the pan and thoroughly mixed in.
6. Over the sausage, pour the eggs into the pan and stir continually with a spatula until they are fully cooked.

Nutrition:

- Kcal: 115 Cal
- Carbs: 6 g
- Protein: 1.4 g

- Prep: 10 minutes
- Serve: 2

Ingredients:

- 2 cored and sliced apples
- water, ½ cup
- maple syrup, 1 tbsp
- ¼ teaspoon of cinnamon, ground
- ¼ teaspoon of ginger, ground
- ½ a squash, cut and peeled.
- A dash of salt

Directions:

1. Cooking spray should be used inside the instant pot.
2. Stir well before adding all the ingredients to the instant pot, excluding the maple syrup.
3. Cook for 8 minutes on high while covering the pot with a lid.
4. Once finished, use quick release to remove pressure. Open the lid.
5. Blend the apple mixture in an immersion blender until smooth after adding the maple syrup and stirring carefully.

Nutrition:

- Kcal: 151 Cal
- Carbs: 39.5 g
- Protein: 1.2 g

- Prep: 10 minutes
- Serve: 4

Ingredients:

- 1 cup of riced cauliflower
- 1 tablespoon finely chopped chives
- Vegetable stock, one cup
- 1 tablespoon minced garlic
- 2 tablespoons of lemon juice, fresh
- 2 cups sliced mushrooms
- 20 ml of olive oil
- halved and quartered grape tomatoes and 1 tiny onion
- spices, salt

Directions:

1. Set the Instant Pot to sauté mode and add oil to the inner pot.
2. Sauté the mushrooms, onion, and garlic for 5 minutes.
3. Stir well after adding the other ingredients.
4. Cook for 15 minutes on high while covering the pot with a lid.
5. Once finished, allow pressure to drop naturally for 10 minutes before using a fast release to release the residual pressure. Open the lid.

Nutrition:

- Kcal: 97 Cal
- Carbs : 6 g
- Protein : 2.7 g

- Prep: 5 minutes
- Serve: 5

Ingredients:

- tablespoon of almond flour
- ¼ tsp xanthan gum with eggs
- 1 parmesan cheese tbsp
- Cheddar cheese, one cup

Directions:

1. The eggs must be beaten in a big bowl. Five tablespoons or so of the remaining ingredients should be added to a baking sheet covered with parchment paper.
2. At 350°F, bake for approximately 12 minutes.
3. Bake for approximately 3 minutes, or until golden brown.

Nutrition:

- Kcal: 119 Cal
- Protein: 7.2 g
- Sodium: 166 mg

Lunch

27. Tuna Salad Sandwich

- **Total Time:** 10 minutes

Main Ingredients:

- 6 ounces of tuna in a can
- 2 lettuce leaves
- 1 ½ teaspoons of sweet pickle relish
- Mayonnaise, 2 ½ tablespoons
- American cheese in two slices.
- bread, four pieces of whole wheat

Directions:

1. Place the tuna in a bowl after it has been drained.
2. Stir the mayonnaise and pickle relish together after adding them.
3. The bread pieces should be toasted in the toaster until both sides are golden brown.
4. Prepare the sandwich by placing a toasted piece of bread on top of a lettuce leaf, followed by half of the tuna salad.

5. A slice of cheese and another toasted bread slice are placed on top of the tuna salad.

6. Create a second sandwich in the same way, then serve it.

Nutrition:

- Kcal: 189.5 Cal; Total Fat: 9.1 g Carbs: 6.1 g; Protein: 20 g;

28. Pepperoni Pizza

- Total Time: 13 minutes

Main Ingredients:

- 8 pepperoni slices
- ½ tsp. dried oregano
- 1/9 cup olive oil
- 2 tablespoons of mozzarella cheese, shredded.
- Pizza sauce, 3 teaspoons
- at room temperature, two eggs

Directions:

1. In a medium bowl, crack the eggs, add the oregano, and whisk to mix.

2. A medium skillet pan should be used. Heat it for 2 minutes on medium heat while adding oil.

3. The egg batter should be poured into the skillet, turned to distribute it uniformly, and cooked for three minutes or until the bottom is solid.

4. After that, place pepperoni slices on top of the omelet, top with cheese, cover the pan with the lid, and cook for two minutes, or until the eggs are set and the cheese has melted.

5. Pizza should be served with pizza sauce after being transferred to a platter.

Nutrition:

- Kcal: 285; Fat: 18 g; Carbs: 8 g; Protein: 22 g;

29. Funny Face Sandwich

- Total Time: 20 minutes

Main Ingredients:

- two pieces of whole grain bread
- 2 substantial, fresh strawberries
- Blueberries, six
- 2/fourths cup peanut butter

Directions:

Kid:

1. Slices of toasted bread should be placed on a cutting board after toasting in a toaster.
2. Each slice of bread should have 1 tablespoon of peanut butter on it.
3. Each strawberry should be divided into three rounds.
4. If strawberries are not available, you can cut three slices from a banana instead.
5. One bread slice should be decorated with two strawberry round slices for the ears and one strawberry square for the nose. The ears should be placed on the upper corners of the bread slice.
6. Put a blueberry for the nose on the strawberry slice, and then place two more blueberries there for the eyes.

Nutrition:

- Kcal: 243; Total Fat: 9.7 g; Carbs: 28.5 g; Protein: 10.3 g;

30. Sandwich on Skewers

- **Total Time:** 10 minutes

Main Ingredients:

- bread, four pieces of whole wheat

- 4 bacon slices
- 4 cheese slices

Directions:

1. Use a cookie cutter of any shape, and then cut out eight bread shapes from the bread slices.
2. Similarly, cut out cheese and bacon shape from cheese and bacon slices.
3. Take a skewer and thread four bread shapes, bacon shapes, and cheese shapes in an alternate position.
4. Assemble another skewer in the same manner and then serve.

Nutritional Information per Serving:

- Kcal: 614.5; Total Fat: 30.7 g; Carbs: 49.2 g; Protein: 35.3 g;

31. Chicken Parmesan Sliders

- Total Time: 30 minutes

Main Ingredients:

- Eight chicken thighs
- half a cup of spiced breadcrumbs
- ¼ cup unsalted butter
- 1 cup of sauce for pasta
- 1 cup of mozzarella cheese, shredded.
- Parmesan cheese, ¼ cup
- Whole-wheat small burger buns, eight

Extra Ingredients:

- salt
- ½ tsp. dry thyme
- ½ tsp. dried basil

Directions:

1. Turn on the oven, then lower the temperature to 400 degrees F and let it warm up.
2. Take a baking sheet, oil it, and then reserve it until needed.
3. In the meantime, combine bread crumbs with salt, thyme, basil, and parmesan cheese in a shallow dish.
4. Melt the butter in a medium bowl in the microwave for one to two minutes.
5. Take a piece of chicken tender, dab it in the melted butter, then roll it in the breadcrumb mixture until it is thoroughly coated.
6. Repeat with the remaining chicken tenders after placing the prepared chicken tender on the prepared baking sheet.
7. Bake the chicken tenders for 15 minutes after placing the baking sheet in the oven.
8. After you're done, take the baking sheet out of the oven and turn on the broiler.
9. Each hamburger bun should be split lengthwise, and the bottom half should be placed on a foil-lined baking sheet.
10. Each burger bun should contain a cooked chicken tender. Add 2 tablespoons of marinara sauce and mozzarella cheese to each chicken tender before covering with the top half of the burger buns.
11. The sandwiches should be broiled until the cheese melts and turns golden brown in the baking dish.

Nutritional Information per Serving:

- Kcal: 500; Total Fat: 20 g; Carbs: 35 g; Protein: 45 g.

- Total Time: 30 minutes

Main Ingredients:

- 2 cups cooked quinoa
- white whole-wheat flour, one-third cup
- ½ cup finely minced white onion
- a tbsp. of minced parsley
- Olive oil, 4 tablespoons
- 1/3 cup of cheddar cheese, shredded.
- at room temperature, three eggs

Extra Ingredients:

- Sea salt, ½ teaspoon
- ½ teaspoon of black pepper, ground

Directions:

Kid:

1. Add the quinoa to a sizable bowl along with the cheese, onion, parsley, salt, and black pepper. Stir to mix.
2. The eggs should be cracked and whisked until smooth before being added to the quinoa mixture and combined.
3. Use a tablespoon or a small ice cream scoop to scoop out portion of the quinoa mixture, roll it into a ball, and then lay the fritter on a dish to prepare the fritters.
4. When ready to cook, add oil to a big skillet and heat it for three minutes over medium heat.
5. After that, add the fritters to the pan and cook them for 3 to 5 minutes on each side, or until golden brown.

6. Fry the fritters, set them on a tray lined with paper towels, and allow them to rest for five minutes.

Nutritional Information per Serving:

- Kcal: 193; Total Fat: 6 g Carbs: 26 g; Protein: 7 g;

33. Quinoa Stuffed Mushrooms

- Cooking Time: 30 minutes| Total Time: 40 minutes

Main Ingredients:

- ½ of a medium white onion, peeled, diced, and 1 cup uncooked quinoa
- Chopped celery, one
- one medium-sized red bell pepper, cored and diced
- Baby spinach leaves in 2 cups
- a single large tomato, diced, and eight Portobello mushroom caps

Extra Ingredients:

- 1/9 cup olive oil
- 1 cup of mozzarella cheese, shredded.
- ¾ cup of water

Directions:

7. Turn on the oven, then lower the temperature to 400 degrees F and let it warm up.
8. Prepare the ingredients by chopping and peeling the onion.
9. The bell pepper should be chopped after being stripped of its stalk and seeds.
10. After chopping the tomato, take the mushrooms' stems out.
11. Once the veggies are evenly coated in oil, add the celery, bell pepper, and onion and sauté for a further 4 minutes, or until fork-tender.
12. Cook for 2 minutes, or until spinach leaves begin to wilt, after adding the tomato and stirring to combine.

13. Turn the heat up to high, whisk in the quinoa, add the water, and then bring the mixture to a boil.

14. Then, bring the heat down to low, cover the pan with its lid, and simmer the quinoa for 10 minutes, or until it is cooked.

15. After incorporating the cheese, remove the pan from heat.

16. Place mushrooms on a baking sheet with a rim that measures 13 by 9 inches. the quinoa mixture, and then fill them.

Nutritional Information per Serving:

- Kcal: 394; Fat: 15 g; Carbs: 42 g Protein: 25 g;

34. Avocado and Cheese Toasties

- Cooking Time: 10 minutes| Total Time: 20 minutes

Main Ingredients:

- a medium avocado, half
- 4 cheddar cheese slices
- 2 tablespoons of unsalted butter
- bread, four pieces of whole wheat

Directions:

Kid:

1. Scoop the avocado's flesh into a bowl and use a fork to mash it.

2. Take two slices of bread, and then butter one side of each with a half-teaspoon.

3. Turn on the sandwich press, place a slice of bread butter-side down inside, and top with half of the mashed avocado.

4. Two cheese slices should be placed on top of the avocado layer before another slice of buttered bread is placed on top and the sandwich press is shut.

5. After the sandwich has cooked until it is golden brown on all sides, place it on a dish.

6. Make a second sandwich in the same way, then serve it.

Nutritional Information per Serving:

- Kcal: 385.8; Fat: 14.4 g; Carbs: 54.5 g; Protein: 12.6 g;

35. Mashed Potato Pancakes

- **Cooking Time:** 15 minutes| **Total Time:** 25 minutes

Main Ingredients:

- three medium potatoes
- 1/4 cup of grated parmesan
- At ambient temperature, one egg
- a cup and a half of white whole-wheat flour
- Olive oil, two tablespoons

Directions:

Kid:

1. Take a medium pot, add the potatoes to it, and then add water until it is 1-inch above the potatoes.
2. The potatoes should be boiled for 15 minutes after being placed in a saucepan over medium-high heat.
3. When a fork readily slides in and out of the potatoes, they have been successfully boiled.
4. The potatoes should then be peeled, cut into slices, and rinsed in cold water.
5. With a fork, mash the potato pieces in a large bowl. Add the egg, cheese, and 3 tablespoons of flour. Stir to mix.
6. Take the remaining flour and put it in a shallow dish.
7. Some of the potato combinations can be scooped out with an ice cream scoop, formed into patties, and then dusted with flour.

8. Repeat with the rest of the potato mixture after placing the potato cake on a dish.
9. Oil should be added to a big skillet before it is heated for 3 minutes at medium heat.
10. Place the potato cakes in the pan and cook for 3 minutes on each side, or until golden.

Nutritional Information per Serving:

- Kcal: 226 Fat: 15 g; Carbs: 19 g; Protein: 3 g;

36. Sweet Potato Wedges

- Cooking Time: 35 minutes| Total Time: 45 minutes

Main Ingredients:

- 4 large, sweet potatoes
- paprika, two tablespoons
- Olive oil, two tablespoons

Directions:

1. Turn on the oven, then lower the temperature to 400 degrees F and let it warm up.
2. Wash the potatoes after scrubbing them and trimming off their ends.
3. Cut each potato into eight wedges by length, one at a time, and put the wedges in a big basin.
4. Toss the wedges in oil and paprika until they are evenly covered. Drizzle oil over the wedges.
5. Take a rimmed baking sheet, arrange the potato wedges in a single layer, and bake for 30 to 35 minutes, rotating them halfway through, until cooked and golden brown.
6. After being finished, allow the wedges to cool for 5 minutes before serving them with a favorite dip.

Nutritional Information per Serving:

- Kcal: 88 Fat: 3 g; Carbs: 13 g; Protein: 1 g;

37. Popcorn Chicken

- Cooking Time: 25 minutes| Total Time: 35 minutes

Main Ingredients:

- 1 pound of skinless chicken breast
- ½ teaspoon of black pepper, ground
- a quarter teaspoon of cayenne
- breadcrumbs, 1 cup.
- Cornmeal, ¼ cup
- At ambient temperature, one egg
- ¼ cup of grated parmesan

Extra Ingredients:

- teaspoon salt

Directions:

1. Turn on the oven, then lower the temperature to 400 degrees F and let it warm up.
2. Grab a baking sheet with a rim. and after that oil to grease it.
3. Chicken should be cut into 1-inch pieces and put in a big basin with salt and pepper. Toss until evenly covered.
4. In a medium bowl, crack the egg, and whisk it until it is well-beaten.
5. In a small bowl, combine the bread crumbs, cornmeal, cheese, salt, and cayenne pepper. Stir to combine.
6. Take a piece of chicken, use a fork to dip it into the egg, then coat it with the bread crumbs mixture before setting it on a baking pan.
7. Repeat with the remaining chicken pieces, arrange them on a baking sheet, and bake for 25 minutes, flipping the chicken over halfway through, until golden brown.

Nutritional Information per Serving:

- Kcal: 351 Fat: 22 g; Carbs: 21 g; Protein: 18 g;

38. Ranch Chicken Tenders

- Cooking Time: 30 minutes| Total Time: 40 minutes

Main Ingredients:

- 1 pound of skinless chicken breast
- White whole-wheat flour, two cups
- 1 regular-sized bag of Doritos in ranch
- ¼ teaspoon each of salt and black pepper
- at room temperature, two eggs

Directions:

1. Turn on the oven, then set the temperature to 350 degrees F, and wait.

2. When not in use, take a baking sheet, line it with parchment paper, and then set it aside.

3. In the meantime, add the Doritos to a food processor and pulse several times to create tiny crumbs.

4. The bag can also be broken with a rolling pin before being placed in a small basin.

5. In a another small bowl, crack the eggs and combine them with a fork.

6. Black pepper, salt, and flour should all be blended in another shallow dish.

7. The chicken should be cut into strips, and each piece should be coated individually with flour, dipped in eggs, and then coated with Doritos before being placed on a baking sheet.

8. Repeat the process with the remaining chicken strips, spacing them apart on the baking sheet.

9. After baking the chicken strips for 30 minutes, rotating them halfway through, until they are soft and golden brown, and then serving.

Nutritional Information per Serving:

- Kcal: 112 Fat: 6.2 g Carbs: 7.1 g; Protein: 7 g;

39. Baked Chicken Meatballs

- Cooking Time: 26 minutes| Total Time: 36 minutes

Main Ingredients:

- 1 pound of chicken meat
- Italian breadcrumbs, ¼ cup
- At ambient temperature, one egg
- ½ cup of finely grated parmesan

Directions:

1. Turn on the oven, then lower the temperature to 400 degrees F and let it warm up.
2. Take a baking sheet with a rim and line it with foil before spritzing it with oil.
3. Take a sizable bowl, add all the ingredients to it, and whisk everything together.
4. Each part of the chicken mixture should be divided into sixteen equal pieces, each measuring approximately 2 tablespoons.
5. Place the meatballs in a single layer on a baking sheet, and bake for 24 to 26 minutes, or until they are well-done and golden brown.

Nutritional Information per Serving:

- Kcal: 200 Fat: 9.4 g; Carbs: 10 g; Protein: 18.4 g;

40. Cheesy Chicken Tacos

- Cooking Time: 22 minutes| Total Time: 32 minutes

Main Ingredients:

- sixteen ounces of refried beans
- 1 medium white onion peeled and chopped, 2 cups cooked and shredded chicken.
- 4.5 ounces of green peppers
- one cup salsa
- 1 ½ cups of chopped Cheese Pepper Jack
- Taco shells: 12

Extra Ingredients:

- 1 salt shakerful
- ½ teaspoon of black pepper, ground
- 1 tablespoon cumin powder
- Olive oil, 1 tbsp

Directions:

1. Turn on the oven, then lower the temperature to 375 degrees F and let it warm up.
2. Oil should be added to a large skillet and heated for 2 minutes at medium heat.
3. Once covered, add the onion and sauté it for 6 minutes or until soft.
4. Stir in the cumin, salt, and black pepper before adding the chicken, green chilies, and salsa.
5. After the chicken has been combined and heated through, remove the pan from the heat.
6. Spread some beans in the shape of a thin layer in a baking dish.
7. The remaining taco shells should be divided between the beans, chicken mixture, and cheese. Bake for 10 minutes, or until the cheese is melted.

Nutritional Information per Serving:

- Kcal: 486 Fat: 14 g; Carbs: 75.6 g; Protein: 17.8 g;

41. Cheesy Rice

- Cooking Time: 12 minutes| Total Time: 17 minutes

Main Ingredients:

- Brown rice, 1 ½ cups
- chopped broccoli florets in 2 cups.
- ½ tsp. of garlic powder
- 4 grains of salt
- 2 tablespoons of unsalted butter
- 1 cup of cheddar cheese, shredded.
- 4 cups of liquid

Directions:

1. A big saucepan should be filled with water and heated to medium. then heat it until it simmers.
2. Rice should be added, cooked for 10 minutes, or until it is soft, drained, and left to stand for 5 minutes.
3. Broccoli florets should be placed in a heatproof bowl, covered with plastic wrap, and microwaved for two minutes or more, or until tender.
4. Drain the broccoli, then add it after adding the rice back into the saucepan.
5. Garlic, salt, butter, and cheese should all be added. Stir until combined.

Nutritional Information per Serving:

- Kcal: 439 Fat: 17.2 g; Carbs: 58.4 g; Protein: 13.2 g;

Soups And Salads

42. Easy Ramen Noodles

- cook time: 10 minutes.

Ingredients

- Vegetable oil, 1 tablespoon
- 1 minced garlic clove
- 1 scallion, root cut off, white and green portions sliced.
- ¼ teaspoon of spicy sauce
- 2 teaspoons soy sauce and 3 cups of vegetable broth
- water, ½ cup
- 1 package (12 ounces) of ramen noodles, with the spice packet discarded.

Preparation

1. To prepare the vegetables, warm the oil in a medium saucepan over medium heat. Add the spicy sauce, scallion, and garlic. Cook the scallions for 2 minutes, or until they start to soften and the white part starts to turn transparent.

2. To make the broth, mix the water, soy sauce, and vegetable broth. Put over medium-high heat and come to a boil. Noodles should be added and cooked for three minutes, or until soft. Pour the soup into two dishes for serving.

Per serving:

- Kcal: 470; total fat: 21g; total carbs: 58g; protein: 11g

43. Chicken Soup

- cook time: 20 minutes.

Ingredients

- Butter, two tablespoons
- ½ chopped yellow onion
- 1 (32-ounce) carton chicken broth, 1 boneless, skinless chicken breast, chopped
- Vegetables in two (14.5-ounce) cans
- Bay leaf, one

Preparation

1. Melt the butter in a medium skillet over medium heat before cooking the chicken. Add the chicken and onion. Cook for about 7 minutes, or until the onion is transparent and the chicken is thoroughly cooked.
2. Produce the soup: Combine the chicken broth, chicken, onion, veggies, and bay leaf in a big pot. Heat to a rolling boil over medium-high. Simmer for 10 minutes, or until cooked thoroughly, on medium-low heat. Get rid of the heat. Before serving, throw away the bay leaf.

Per serving:

- Kcal: 164; total fat: 5g; total carbs: 18g; protein: 13g

- cook time: 20 minutes

Ingredients

- Vegetable oil, 1 tablespoon
- 1 minced tiny onion
- 2 minced garlic cloves
- Chop one medium jalapeo pepper after seeding it.
- 5 cans (14.5 ounces each) of chicken broth
- Diced tomatoes in two (14.5-ounce) cans.
- 1 pound of cooked, shredded chicken and ½ teaspoon salt
- 1 medium-ripe avocado
- tortilla corn chips
- Monterey Jack cheese, grated into a half cup
- wedges sliced from 1 lime

Preparation

1. To prepare the veggies, heat the oil in a large saucepan over medium-high heat. Add the onion, and sauté it for two minutes, or until it begins to become translucent, while stirring regularly. Add the jalapeo and garlic. Cook for 2 to 3 minutes, stirring regularly, or until aromatic.
2. Produce the soup: Add salt, chicken, tomatoes, and broth while stirring. up to a boil. Medium-low heat should be reduced, the lid should be on, and the chicken should simmer for 15 minutes or until well heated.
3. Serve: Peel and pit the avocado before serving. Slice it into one-inch pieces. The tortilla chips should be divided among 4 serving bowls. Place a bowl of soup in each. Add avocado and cheese to each plate, then top with more tortilla chips as a garnish. slices of lime are optional.

Per serving:

- Kcal: 479; total fat: 51g; total carbs: 21g; protein: 51g

45. Chicken and Dumplings

- cook time: 25 minutes

Ingredients

- Butter, two tablespoons
- 1/2 yellow onion, chopped finely
- 1 cup of carrots, chopped
- 1 pound of cooked chicken, chopped, 2 celery stalks, chopped, and 4 cups of chicken broth
- Condensed cream of chicken soup, 1 (10.5-ounce) can
- quarter teaspoon of freshly ground pepper
- Frozen peas, 1 cup
- 1/9 cup all-purpose flour
- 1 (16.3 ounce) tube of chilled cookies

Preparation

1. Melt the butter in a sizable saucepan over medium-high heat before preparing the chicken and vegetables. Add the chicken, onion, carrots, and celery. Cook the onion until it turns translucent, which takes about 5 minutes.
2. Produce the soup: Mix the soup, broth, and pepper in a large mixing bowl. Chicken and veggies should be added. up to a boil. Medium-low heat should be used. Add the peas, cover, and boil for 5 minutes while stirring regularly.
3. Creating the dumplings: A cutting board should be covered in flour. Use the palm of a clean hand to press each biscuit until it is 1/4 inch thick. Cut each biscuit into four pieces. Drop a biscuit into the broth one at a time. The biscuits should be fluffy and cooked through after 15 minutes of simmering under cover with occasional tossing. Get rid of the heat.

Per serving:

- Kcal: 417; total fat: 11g; total carbs: 46g; protein: 33g

46. Almost Homemade Tomato Soup

- cook time: 10 minutes

Ingredients

- spaghetti sauce made with tomatoes and basil, one (26-ounce) jar.
- 3 cups full-fat cream
- 1 ½   tablespoons of Worcestershire sauce and ½ cup sugar
- Shredded fresh basil is used as a garnish.

Preparation

1. Produce the soup: A medium saucepan should now contain the pasta sauce. Add the cream and blend. Worcestershire sauce and sugar are added. Combine by whisking. Warm up the mixture and dissolve the sugar over medium heat (do not boil). Get rid of the heat.

2. Serve: Pour the soup into 4 bowls, then sprinkle basil on top.

3. Theme It Up: For a classy finishing touch, toast a slice of robust bread (sourdough works well), tear it into bite-sized pieces, and place it in the middle of each bowl.

4. Another suggestion is to purée the spaghetti sauce in the blender before adding it to the pot to make the soup smoother.

Per serving:

- Kcal: 756; fat: 66g; carbs: 40g; 33g; protein: 6g

- cook time: 20 minutes

Ingredients

- 1/9 cup olive oil
- 1 cup of vegetable broth, 1 celery stalk, 1 large carrot, 1 minced garlic clove, and ½ a small onion
- Italian-seasoned chopped tomatoes in a single 14.5-ounce can
- boiled elbow pasta, ¼ cup
- ¼ teaspoon freshly ground pepper and 1/2 teaspoon salt

Preparation

1. Get the vegetables ready: Heat the oil in a medium saucepan over a medium flame. Include the carrot, celery, and onion. Cook for 10 minutes, stirring once or twice, or until the veggies are soft. Stir after adding the garlic.
2. Produce the soup: Add the tomato, pasta, and broth. Add salt and pepper to taste. Simmer for 10 minutes or until thoroughly heated. Get rid of the heat.

Per serving:

- Kcal: 135; total fat: 3g; total carbs: 23g; protein: 3g

48. Broccoli-Cheese Soup

- cook time: 30 minutes

Ingredients

- Butter, two tablespoons
- ½ cup finely sliced yellow onion
- 2 tablespoons of regular flour
- 3-gallon milk
- 2 cups of cooked, chopped broccoli in 1 cup of vegetable broth.
- Julienned carrots in a cup

- 2 cups of cheese, Cheddar, shredded
- Salt
- black pepper freshly ground
- ½ tsp. sour cream

Preparation

1. To make a roux, melt the butter in a large pot over medium heat. Put the onion in. Cook until tender, about 5 minutes. Add the flour and mix. After about a minute, add the milk and vegetable broth gently, about 14 cup at a time, and whisk until smooth and thick.
2. Produce the soup: Include the carrots and broccoli. About 10 minutes, or until heated thoroughly and the flavors are blended, should be spent simmering. The cheese should completely melt and mingle in about 10 minutes of cooking after being stirred in. Add salt and pepper to taste. Get rid of the heat.

Per serving:

- Kcal: 424; total fat: 29g; total carbs: 21g; protein: 22g

49. Vegetarian Chili

- cook time: 40 minutes.

Ingredients

- Vegetable oil, two tablespoons
- 2 (14.5 ounce) cans diced tomatoes, chopped 1 yellow onion, chopped 2 (15 ounce) cans dark red kidney beans, drained and rinsed
- Chili powder, two tablespoons
- two salty teaspoons

Preparation

1. To make the chili, warm the oil in a big pot over medium heat. When the onion is transparent, add it and simmer for about 5 minutes. Add the beans, salt, chili powder, and tomatoes together with their liquid.
2. Stirring sporadically, simmer for 30 minutes, or until well cooked and the flavors have melded. Get rid of the heat.

Per serving:

- Kcal: 194; total fat: 6g; total carbs: 29g; protein: 9g

50. Chicken Chili

- cook time: 30 minutes

Ingredients

- 1 breast of chicken
- 2 tablespoons of olive oil, divided, and a further ½ teaspoon of salt as needed
- black pepper freshly ground
- 1 minced garlic clove and 12 tiny onion
- 1 chopped tiny red bell pepper
- ½ tsp. dried basil

- ¼ tsp. chili powder
- ¼ teaspoon of cumin, ground
- 1 can (15 oz) of diced tomatoes
- 1 (15-ounce) can of rinsed and drained red kidney beans

Preparation

1. Turn the oven on to 400 degrees and bake the chicken. Apply 1 tablespoon of oil on the chicken with a pastry brush, then season with salt and pepper. In an 8 by 8 inch baking pan, place the chicken. Bake for 15 to 18 minutes, or until the internal temperature reaches 165°F, after transferring to the oven. From the oven, remove. Transfer the chicken to a cutting board and chop once it is cold enough to handle.

2. Get the vegetables ready: In the meantime, heat the final tablespoon of oil in a medium skillet over low heat. When the onion is transparent, add it and simmer for another 7 to 9 minutes. When the garlic is aromatic, add it and stir for 30 seconds. Add the salt, cumin, chili powder, basil, and bell pepper. Cook for one minute while stirring until aromatic. tomato dice are added. After bringing to a boil, turn the heat down to medium-low. Cook for 15 minutes, or until well cooked and the flavors have combined.

3. Add the chicken and beans to the chili to make it. Stirring often, simmer for 5 minutes or until thoroughly heated. Pour the chili into a bowl and top with sour cream and cheese, if desired (if using).

Per serving:

- Kcal: 453; total fat: 18g; total carbs: 46g; protein: 32g

- cook time: 15 minutes

Ingredients

- 8 cups of chicken stock
- one sliced onion
- 1 chopped jalapeno pepper
- 2 chopped garlic cloves
- 1 teaspoon cumin, 2 teaspoons lime zest
- 28 peeled shrimp
- 2 limes juice
- Salt, 1/2 teaspoon
- Hot sauce dash
- 2 avocados, peeled, pitted, and diced, and 1 cup chopped tomatoes.

Preparation

1. Produce the soup: Combine the chicken broth, onion, jalapenos, garlic, lime zest, and cumin in a medium pot.
2. Let the ingredients combine and heat through for 10 minutes. Add the spicy sauce, lime juice, salt, and shrimp.
3. Cook the shrimp for three minutes, or until they turn pink. Get rid of the heat. The tomatoes and avocados have been added. If using, garnish with cilantro and serve with lime wedges (if using).

Per serving:

- Kcal: 337; total fat: 45g; total carbs: 15g; protein: 33g

- cook time: 30 minutes

Ingredients

- Italian sausage in quantity, 1 pound
- Red pepper flakes, 1/4 to 1/2 teaspoon
- 1 cup of onion, chopped
- 14-inch thick slices of two huge russet potatoes, sliced into halves.
- Chicken broth in a can (14.5 ounces).
- Water in 4 glasses
- 2 minced garlic cloves
- 1 cup of chopped cooked bacon
- Salt
- black pepper freshly ground
- 2 cups of kale, chopped
- heavy cream, 1 cup

Preparation

1. Prepare the meat and veggies by browning the sausage in a medium skillet over medium heat for about 5 minutes. Red pepper flakes are added. The sausage should be cooked thoroughly for an additional 2 minutes on each side. Get rid of the heat. Combine the onion, potatoes, chicken broth, water, and garlic in a big pot. Over medium heat, bring to a boil. Cook the potatoes for approximately 10 minutes, or until they are tender.

2. Produce the soup: Sausage and bacon have been added. Add salt and pepper to taste. Reduce the heat to low and simmer for 10 minutes, or until the flavors blend. Add the cream and kale. Cook for approximately 10 minutes, or until thoroughly cooked (do not boil). Get rid of the heat.

Per serving:

- Kcal: 434; total fat: 34g; total carbs: 25g; protein: 17g

53. French Onion Soup

- cook time: 1 hour 35 minutes

Ingredients

- 4 cups of onions, thinly sliced
- Divided, 8 tablespoons (1 stick) of butter
- 1/4 teaspoon freshly ground pepper 1 teaspoon sugar
- beef stock, 6 cups
- 1 teaspoon of salt
- 4 pieces of French bread, each 1 inch thick
- split into 14 cup, 1 ½ tablespoons of grated Parmesan cheese
- 1 ½ cups of Gruyère cheese, shredded

Preparation

1. To caramelize the onions, melt 4 tablespoons of butter in a 5- to 6-quart heavy-bottomed pot over medium heat. Include the onions. Toss to spread the butter on them. Cook for 15 to 20 minutes, stirring frequently, or until soft. Heat up the food to a medium-high level. Add the sugar and the remaining 4 tablespoons of butter. Cook for about 15 minutes, stirring frequently, or until the onions begin to brown. Add some pepper for flavor.

2. To make the broth, heat the beef stock over medium-high heat in a medium saucepan. Add salt and onions. For an hour, or until the flavors combine, simmer gently with the lid on over medium-low heat. Get rid of the heat.

3. Get the bread ready: Pre-heat the oven to 450°F about 15 minutes before the broth is done. Use aluminum foil to cover a baking sheet. Brush the bread with 34 cup oil before placing it on the baking sheet. Toast the baking sheet for 5 to 7 minutes, or until lightly browned, on the middle rack of the oven. The

bread should be turned over, brushed with the final 1/4 teaspoon of oil, and sprinkled with Parmesan cheese. Go back to the oven and toast the bread for an additional two minutes. From the oven, remove.

Per serving:

- Kcal: 590; total fat: 42g; total carbs: 32g; protein: 24g

54. Cucumber Salad

- Prep time: 10 minutes

Ingredients

- 1 chopped and peeled cucumber
- a single sliced and corer tomato
- finely chopped half a cup of vinaigrette dressing and one tiny red onion

Preparation

1. To make the salad, put the cucumber, tomato, and onion in a medium mixing basin. Vinaigrette dressing added; toss to combine. Add sesame seeds on top (if using).

Per serving:

- Kcal: 162; total fat: 9gtotal carbs: 16g; protein: 2g

55. Tuna Salad

- Prep time: 5 minutes

Ingredients

- 1 (7-ounce), drained tuna can
- ¼ teaspoon freshly ground pepper and ½ teaspoon salt
- ½ cup of mayonnaise

Preparation

1. To prepare the tuna salad, flake the tuna with a fork in a medium mixing basin. Add salt and pepper to taste. With two forks, add the mayonnaise and gently stir.

Per serving:

- Kcal: 238; total fat: 20g; total carbs: 0g; protein: 13g

56. Macaroni Salad

- Prep time: 15 minutes

Ingredients

- 5 cups chilled cooked elbow macaroni
- 1 (4-ounce) container of chopped pimientos
- ¾ cup mayonnaise and 1 cup diced celery
- a tablespoon of onion, minced
- Green bell pepper, minced, 1 tbsp
- freshly squeezed lemon juice, 1 tbsp
- ¼ teaspoon paprika, 1 ½ tablespoons salt

Preparation

1. To make the salad, combine the macaroni, pimientos, celery, mayonnaise, onion, bell pepper, lemon juice, salt, and paprika in a sizable mixing basin. Lightly stir with a fork until combined.

Per serving:

- Kcal: 394; total fat: 21g; total carbs: 43g; protein: 8g

- Prep time: 10 minutes

Ingredients

- florets from two broken broccoli heads
- 12 ounces of dried cranberries
- 1 small red onion, diced, and ½ cup of drained mandarin orange slices
- ½ cup of plain yogurt
- Sugar, ¼ cup
- vinegar, 1 tablespoon
- 12 pieces of cooked bacon, crumbled, or Easy Crispy Oven bacon.

Preparation

1. To make the salad, put the broccoli, dried cranberries, onion, and mandarin oranges in a medium mixing basin.
2. Creating the dressing Combine the yogurt, sugar, and vinegar in a small mixing dish. until smooth, stir. Mix the salad after adding the dressing, coating the broccoli completely. Serve the salad with the bacon on top.

Per serving:

- Kcal: 493; total fat: 25g; total carbs: 41g; protein: 28g

58. Chicken Taco Salad

- cook time: 10 minutes.

Ingredients

- a single skinless, boneless chicken breast
- ¼ cup taco seasoning
- 10 grams of butter
- Corn kernels, ¼ cup.
- Ranch dressing, 1/3 cup.

- 8 ml of salsa
- 1 ½ teaspoons freshly minced cilantro
- 1 cup shredded green leaf lettuce.
- 1 diced Roma tomato
- ¼ cup of pepper jack cheese, grated.
- 1 avocado, chopped after being pitted.

Preparation

1. Chicken preparation: Taco seasoning is used to season the chicken. Melt the butter over medium-high heat in a large skillet. Cook the chicken for 4 minutes on each side, or until the internal temperature reaches 165°F, after adding it to the pan. Chicken should be taken off of the skillet. Reduce the heat to medium-low, add the corn to the skillet, and cook, stirring regularly, for 2 minutes or until the corn is beginning to brown. Get rid of the heat.
2. Creating the dressing Combine the ranch dressing, salsa, and cilantro mince in a small mixing bowl.
3. assemble the salad: Cut up the chicken. Place the lettuce, chicken, tomato, cheese, corn, and avocado in a serving bowl. On top of the salad, drizzle the dressing. Enjoy.

Per serving:

- Kcal: 790; total fat: 50g; total carbs: 52g; protein: 42g

59. Beef Taco Layer Salad

- cook time: 30 minutes

Ingredients

- 1 ½ pounds of ground pork
- 1 pack of seasoning for tacos
- 1 (8-ounce) sour cream container

- 1 package (8 ounces) of cream cheese
- one salsa cup
- ½ head of shredded iceberg lettuce
- a single, chopped big yellow onion
- 4 ounces of pickled jalapenos in a can (optional)
- 1 pound of shredded mild Cheddar cheese
- 2 chopped ripe tomatoes

Preparation

1. To prepare the meat, brown the beef in a medium skillet over medium heat for about 7 minutes. After draining the beef, properly get rid of the oil. Stir the beef with the taco seasoning after combining it as directed on the packet. The mixture should thicken and the liquid should evaporate after 15 to 20 minutes of simmering. Get rid of the heat. Allow to reach room temperature.
2. Making the sauce: Use an electric mixer to thoroughly blend the sour cream, cream cheese, and salsa in a medium mixing basin.
3. Salad is layered: In a 9 by 13-inch baking dish, layer all the ingredients and top with chips.

Per serving:

- Kcal: 725; total fat: 54g; total carbs: 26g; protein: 35g

Desserts:

60. Hot Fudge Ice Cream Dessert

- Serve: 6 Serve.

Ingredients:

- one cup of little marshmallows
- quarter cup evaporated milk
- Semisweet chocolate chips, half a cup
- Butterscotch chips, 1/4 cup.
- Milk chocolate chips, 1/4 cup.
- ten vanilla wafers
- 1 quart of softened butter pecan ice cream
- 9 toasted pecan halves
- Maraschino cherries, four

Directions:

1. In a saucepan, combine the chips, milk, and marshmallows to make fudge sauce. Cook and stir the mixture slowly over low heat until it melts. Remove from heat and chill in the refrigerator.
2. The bottom of a 6-inch springform pan should be lined with vanilla wafers. 1 cup of ice cream should be added and pressed down to create a smooth layer.
3. Top with a third of the fudge sauce. for about 30 minutes, freeze until frozen. After each layer, freeze, then repeat these steps twice.
4. On top, scatter pecans and cherries. Cover, then freeze until solid. Ten to fifteen minutes before serving, remove from the freezer.

Nutrition:

- Kcal: 501 Cal
- Total Carbohydrate: 55 g
- Total Fat: 30 g
- Protein: 8 g

61. Raspberry Hot Fudge Sundae

- Serve: 6-8

Ingredients:

- Frozen raspberries, 1 ½ cups (without syrup)
- 1-quart softened vanilla ice cream
- Sauce for raspberries: 1 cup sugar
- water, ¼ cup.
- raspberries, 3 cups (without syrup)
- Warm Toffee Sauce:
- 2/3 cup milk
- ¼ cup of butter
- 4 grains of salt
- 2 cups (12 oz.) Chips of semisweet chocolate

- Vanilla extract, 1 teaspoon
- Almond cream whipped topping:
- 1 cup heavy cream for whipping
- almond essence, 1 teaspoon

Directions:

1. Gently fold the raspberries into the vanilla ice cream before placing in a freezer container with a cover and freezing until stiff.
2. In a 2-qt. saucepan, combine sugar and water; bring to a boil over medium heat for one minute. Turn off the heat and give it 15 minutes to cool. Raspberries can be added to the mixture gently and then chilled.
3. Salt, butter, and milk should be combined in a double boiler's top over warm (not boiling) water to form the fudge sauce. Add the chocolate and whisk until the chips are melted and the mixture is smooth after heating until the butter has melted. Turn off the heat and stir in the vanilla.
4. Just before serving, beat the cream until it forms soft peaks, then stir in the almond essence. 2-3 tablespoons of each sauce should be placed on top of the ice cream in a sizable sundae bowl or dessert plate. Garnish with a dollop of whipped topping.

Nutrition:

- Kcal: 633 Cal
- Total Carbohydrate: 76 g
- Protein: 6 g

62. Homemade Peach Ice Cream

- Serve: 2

Ingredients:

- 1 cup softened vanilla ice cream.
- 2.3 cups of sliced unsweetened frozen peaches
- 8 ml of vanilla extract
- Cinnamon, ground, a dash

Directions:

1. The peach, ice cream, vanilla, cinnamon, and spices should all be added to a blender and blended until smooth. Pour the mixture into small dessert dishes that may be frozen, cover, and serve.

Nutrition:

- Kcal: 158 Cal
- Total Carbohydrate: 22 g
- Protein: 3 g

63. Choco Rice Pudding

- Serve: 4

Ingredients:

- ¼ cup of rice
- ¼ cup chopped dark chocolate.
- 1 teaspoon vanilla
- 1/3 cup coconut oil
- liquid stevia, 1 teaspoon
- 2 ½ cups of almond milk

Directions:

1. Stir everything well before adding it to the inner pot of the instant pot.
2. Cook for 20 minutes on high while covering the pot with a lid.
3. Once finished, permit pressure to escape normally. Open the lid.

Nutrition:

- Kcal 632 Cal
- Carbs 63.5 g
- Protein 8.6 g

64. Chocolate Rice

- Serve: 4

Ingredients:

- 1 serving of rice
- 1-tablespoon cocoa powder
- 2/batch of maple syrup
- 2 glasses of almond milk

Directions:

1. Stir everything well before adding it to the inner pot of the instant pot.
2. Cook for 20 minutes on high while covering the pot with a lid.
3. Once finished, allow pressure to drop naturally for 10 minutes before using a fast release to release the residual pressure. Open the lid.

Nutrition:

- Kcal 474 Cal
- Carbs 51.1 g
- Protein 6.3 g

- Serve: 4

Ingredients:

- 1 (16 ounce) container of drained silken tofu
- 1.5 cups of pure maple syrup
- Pure vanilla extract, 1 teaspoon
- ¼ cup of soy milk
- unsweetened cocoa powder, half a cup

Directions:

1. Blend or process the tofu, maple syrup, and vanilla in a food processor. Blend thoroughly after processing.
2. When the mixture is well combined, add the other ingredients and process once more.
3. at least two hours to chill.
4. Just before serving, add fresh mint leaves as a garnish.

Nutrition:

- Kcal: 259 Cal
- Carbs: 14 g
- Protein: 7 g

- Serve: 16+ squares

Ingredients:

- 1 cup chopped Medjool dates, 2 tablespoons heated coconut oil, and ½ cup peanut butter.
- unsweetened cocoa powder, ¼ cup
- ½ cup of walnuts
- a single vanilla bean.

Directions:

1. For 20 to 30 minutes, soak the dates in warm water.
2. Coconut oil should be used to lightly grease an 8" square baking pan.
3. Dates, peanut butter, cocoa powder, and vanilla should all be added to a food processor and smoothed up.
4. Add walnuts and fold.
5. When the fudge is nice and stiff, pack it into the oiled baking pan and freeze it for an hour.
6. Slice into 16 or more bite-sized squares, then put them in a refrigerator container with a loose lid.

Nutrition:

- Kcal: 120 Cal
- Carbs: 19 g
- Protein: 3 g

- Serve: 4-6

Ingredients:

- Medjool dates, ¼ cup
- All-purpose flour, 1 ¼ cups
- two tablespoons of baking powder
- ¼ tsp. baking soda
- Salt, ½ teaspoon
- ½ cup sugar
- milk, ¼ cup
- 1 gently beaten egg.
- 1 tablespoon grated orange peel
- ¼ cup of buckwheat flour and 1 tbsp of heated coconut oil
- 1 cup chopped walnuts.

Directions:

1. On a cutting board, arrange the dates and cover them with 1 tablespoon of all-purpose flour. Dates should be finely chopped after being dipped into flour. To prevent the chopped fruit from clinging to one another, flour the knife frequently.
2. Sift into a large bowl the remaining All-Purpose flour, baking powder, baking soda, salt, and sugar.
3. The milk, egg, orange peel, and oil should all be combined in a different bowl.
4. Then, gently fold in the dates, any flour that is still on the cutting board, and the walnuts after adding the buckwheat flour and thoroughly combining the two mixtures of flour.
5. Add the liquid ingredients, then stir just until incorporated.

6. Put the dough in a baking dish that has been greased and floured. Put the slow cooker in the cover. To let steam out, prop the crockpot lid open a tiny bit with a toothpick or a small piece of twisted aluminum foil.

7. For 4 to 6 hours, cook on high. Cool for ten minutes on a rack. cold or warm serving.

8. Whenever the bread is baking, DO NOT lift the crockpot cover.

Nutrition:

- Kcal: 70 Cal
- Carbs: 15 g
- Protein: 1 g

68. Strawberry Rhubarb Crisp

- Serve: 6-8

Ingredients:

- sugar, white, one cup
- 3 tablespoons plus ½ cup buckwheat flour
- Sliced strawberries, diced rhubarb, and juice from half a lemon are combined with one cup of packed brown sugar.
- 1 cup melted coconut oil, ¼ cup rolled oats.
- ¼ cup chopped walnuts and ¼ cup buckwheat groats.

Directions:

1. Turn on the 375°F oven.
2. Combine white sugar, 3 tablespoons flour, strawberries, rhubarb, and lemon juice in a sizable bowl. The ingredients should be put in a 9 x 13 baking dish.
3. Mix 12 cup flour, brown sugar, coconut oil, oats, buckwheat groats, and walnuts in another bowl until crumbly. For this, a pastry blender might be useful. Top the strawberry and rhubarb mixture with crumble.

4. Bake for 45 minutes, or until crisp and gently browned, in a preheated oven.

Nutrition:

- Kcal: 240 Cal
- Carbs: 42 g
- Protein: 2 g

69. Chocolate Maple Walnuts

- Serve: 2

Ingredients:

- 2 cups of raw, whole walnuts and half a cup of pure maple syrup
- 5 squares of at least 85% dark chocolate
- 1 ½ tablespoons of melted coconut oil
- a single tablespoon of water
- With icing sugar sifted
- Vanilla extract, 1 teaspoon

Directions:

1. Using parchment paper, line a sizable baking sheet.
2. The walnuts and 1/4 cup of maple syrup should be combined in a medium- to large-sized skillet. Cook over medium heat, turning constantly, until the walnuts are completely covered in syrup and brown in color, about 3 to 5 minutes.
3. Use a fork to break up the walnuts as you pour them onto the parchment paper. Give the mixture at least 15 minutes to totally cool.
4. Melt the chocolate and coconut oil in a double boiler while waiting. Stir in all of the leftover maple syrup after adding it.
5. Transfer the cooled walnuts to a glass bowl, then cover them with the melted chocolate syrup. Gently combine with a silicone spatula until all of the walnuts are covered.

6. Return to the baking sheet that has been lined with parchment paper and use a fork to once again separate each nut.

7. Until the chocolate is completely set, place the nuts in the refrigerator for 10 minutes or the freezer for 3–5 minutes.

8. Keep in your refrigerator in an airtight bag.

Nutrition:

- Kcal:155 Cal
- Carbs: 18 g
- Protein: 2 g

70. Chocolate Chip Cookies

- Serve: 16

Ingredients:

- 1.5 cups of flour
- Cornstarch, one tablespoon
- one tablespoon of baking soda
- ¼ cup salt
- 1 cup vegan butter
- ¾ cup of brown sugar
- ¼ cup water, ¼ cup sugar
- 1 tablespoon of vanilla extract purified.
- 12 tablespoons of vegan chocolate chips

Directions:

1. Heat the oven to 350 °F. 2 or 3 big cookie sheets should be lined with parchment.

2. In a larger basin, mash together the flour, cornstarch, salt, and baking soda. Place aside.

3. Beat the margarine, brown sugar, sugar, water, and vanilla until frothy using a mixer or by hand. Slowly incorporate into the flour mixture.
4. Add the chocolate chips and nuts after the flour mixture has been combined.
5. Place about 2 inches between each tablespoon of spherical dough as you ladle it into the prepared pan.
6. Bake for 10–12 minutes, or until the edges are crisp-golden. Serve after letting it cool in the pan.

Nutrition:

- Kcal: 171 Cal
- Carbs: 22 g
- Protein: 2.5 g

Conclusion

Finally, "Teens Cookbook" embarks on a tantalizing voyage that encourages young people to strike out on their culinary explorations with courage and originality. This book's pages have covered a wide range of fundamental cooking skills, delicious recipes, and helpful advice catered specifically to the tastes and requirements of teenagers. This cookbook has worked to foster not only the passion for food but also the sense of satisfaction that comes from making a delectable meal from scratch. It offers quick and nutritious breakfast options as well as hearty feasts that bring friends and families together.

We now understand that cooking is an art form that promotes experimentation and self-expression in addition to being a useful skill. As aspiring cooks, you now have the means to play around with flavors, modify recipes to suit your tastes, and even produce culinary masterpieces. Keep in mind that every meal presents a chance for growth—both in the kitchen and beyond. You'll be glad you learned these abilities as you set out on your path to independence and adulthood.

These dishes offer a feeling of satisfaction and joy, whether you're cooking up a hearty bowl of pasta, grilling a juicy burger, or indulging in a sweet treat. Beyond the mouthwatering recipes, this book aims to instill responsibility, time management, and nutrition knowledge—the cornerstones of a healthier and more well-rounded living.

Remember that cooking is a lifelong talent that develops alongside you as you put "Teens Cookbook" to bed. Continue experimenting, utilizing fresh ingredients, and delighting loved ones with your culinary creations. You nurture more than just your body with each meal you prepare; you also build relationships, cherish memories, and appreciate the bounty of life.

So here's to your culinary journey, which I hope will be full of humor, inventiveness, and the mouthwatering smells of excellent cuisine. May your pots always boil with ambition, your pans always sizzle with zeal, and your plates always display the colorful mosaic of flavors that genuinely distinguish your cuisine.

Printed in Great Britain
by Amazon

39661563R00057